21st Century Skills Library

21ˢᵗ
Century
Skills Library

COOL CAREERS

INTERPRETER

TAMRA B. ORR

Published in the United States of America by
Cherry Lake Publishing, Ann Arbor, Michigan
www.cherrylakepublishing.com

Content Adviser

Anabel Aliaga-Buchenau, Associate Professor of German and Comparative Literature,
University of North Carolina at Charlotte

Credits

Photos: Cover and page 1, ©AP Photo/Marty Lederhandler; page 4, ©Jim West/
Alamy; page 7, ©david pearson/Alamy; page 9, ©The London Art Archive/Alamy;
page 11, ©Philip Wolmuth/Alamy; page 12, ©Nob50/Dreamstime.com; page 14,
©Robert Fried/Alamy; page 16, ©Michaeljung/Dreamstime.com; page 18, ©Image
Source Pink/Alamy; page 20, ©AP Photo/Emile Wamsteker; page 23, ©AP Photo/Ron
Edmonds; page 24, ©Paul David Drabble/Alamy; page 25, ©AP Photo/AP Photo;
page 27, ©AP Photo/Bassem Tellawi.

Library of Congress Cataloging-in-Publication Data

Orr, Tamra.
  Interpreter / by Tamra B. Orr.
      p. cm.—(Cool careers)
  Includes index.
  ISBN-13: 978-1-60279-498-6
  ISBN-10: 1-60279-498-7
  1. Translating and interpreting—Vocational guidance. 2. Translators.
I. Title. II. Series.
  P306.6.O77 2009
  418'.02023—dc22   2008046826

Cherry Lake Publishing would like to acknowledge
the work of The Partnership for 21st Century Skills.
Please visit *www.21stcenturyskills.org* for more information.

TABLE OF CONTENTS

CHAPTER ONE

HELPING PEOPLE TALK TO EACH OTHER

Karl took a deep breath. He had been sitting in the doctor's waiting room for two hours. He had practiced what he was going to say a hundred times. But he was still

Interpreters can help make going to the doctor's office less stressful for people who don't speak English.

afraid that he would make a mistake. Karl had moved to the United States 3 months earlier. Although he was learning more English every day, he still struggled to speak. If he could only tell the doctor in German what he needed, he would be fine.

"Karl Schmidt?" a nurse called out, looking around the crowded office.

Karl jumped up and followed her as she began asking questions. He was already lost. The nurse glanced at his file and then said, "I will be right back."

Worried that he had done something wrong, Karl paced. There was a knock at the door and another woman came in. "Karl Schmidt?" she asked. "*Mein Name ist Katherine. Wie kann ich Ihnen helfen*? (My name is Katherine. What can I do for you?)"

Karl grinned. He couldn't believe it! This woman spoke German perfectly. In just a few minutes, he was able to explain that he needed refills on his medication. He had run out, and his medical doctor was in Germany. He needed a new doctor. Katherine reassured him that it would not be a problem. Karl sighed with relief.

"*Danke*! (Thank you!)" he said. "*Woher aus Deutschlands kommen Sie*? (What part of Germany are you from?)" he asked her.

Katherine laughed. She was from Provo, Utah! She was the medical center's interpreter. It was her job to help patients who did not speak English communicate with their doctors. She knew four languages: German, French, Spanish, and English. Karl was impressed. He was also grateful—she had certainly made his life easier!

Interpreters like Katherine help people every single day. By knowing at least two languages very well, they can help translate one language into another. This way, people are able to communicate with each other. People have been doing this job for centuries.

How far back interpreting goes in history is unclear. The first proof experts have dates back to 3000 BCE. The ancient Egyptians used a sign called a **hieroglyph** to show a person who appeared to be an interpreter.

In ancient Greece and Rome, the slaves and prisoners were the people who knew many languages. The higher classes felt that learning the languages of the cultures they had conquered was improper.

Religion helped to spread interpreting. People from one area would travel to another to share and teach the basics of their faith to others. Trade between countries also increased the need for interpreters.

Exploring the world also meant experiencing new languages. In the early 16th century, a woman named Doña Marina worked with Spanish explorer and **conquistador** Hernán Cortés. She helped him communicate with the natives he met during his conquests. Sacagawea, another

Visitors to the British Museum look at the Rosetta Stone. The ancient Egyptian artifact helped experts figure out how to read hieroglyphs.

famous interpreter, traveled with Meriwether Lewis and William Clark. She helped translate the explorers' words to the Native American tribes they met.

Interpreters were used for many reasons during the early 20th century. But it wasn't until 1945 that many people began to pay attention to them. This happened during a series of famous trials known as the Nuremberg war crimes trials. Many of the people involved in the trials were German. Interpreters were brought into the courtroom to translate questions and answers.

In the 1970s, the interest in interpreting began growing in the United States. Special schools for foreign language training opened. Today, the field is growing quickly. There are people from many different cultures living in the United States. International business is growing. For these and other reasons, the need for people who understand more than one language is soaring. Interpreters are needed in many places including:

- banks
- colleges and universities
- computer industry
- corporations
- courtrooms
- government agencies
- immigration services
- medical offices and hospitals
- military groups
- travel industry

During the Nuremburg trials, people listened to interpreters through headphones.

LIFE & CAREER SKILLS

Interpreters deal with spoken language. Translators work only with written language. They translate books and other written materials from one language to another.

Interpreters and translators must know at least two languages. They must speak them as well as someone born in a country where people speak the language. This means knowing each language's specific slang, common phrases, and odd sayings. Interpreters and translators also usually develop a specialty, such as Internet technology or marketing.

What can you do to become fluent in a foreign language? One way is to live in the foreign country for a while. Can you think of any other ways to develop fluency in a foreign language?

Interpreters help people communicate with one another. They are there to make things easier and more comfortable for everyone.

Interpreters can help make moving to a new country a little easier.

CHAPTER TWO
OFF TO WORK!

Sally Sanders's telephone rang. She ran to answer it. It was the interpreting agency she worked for. Sally is a Japanese interpreter. She usually works in medical offices to help patients understand their doctors. She wrote down

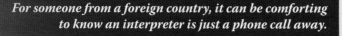

For someone from a foreign country, it can be comforting to know an interpreter is just a phone call away.

some information, hung up the phone, and drove to a medical clinic. When she arrived, she showed her identification to the receptionist at the front desk.

A patient arrived after a few minutes. The nurse introduced him to Sally. Together, they went in to speak with the doctor. "I listen very carefully and then try to give the patient a word-for-word translation of what each person says," explained Sally. "They ask questions, and I make sure they are both satisfied that they are being heard." When the appointment was over, Sally recorded information on a time slip. She would need to turn that in at her agency in order to get paid.

Working in the medical world can be tense. "In many cases, patients are stressed and can't understand what is happening to them," she said. "They are often extremely grateful to have someone who speaks their language. They feel empowered by my presence. It is an emotional bond that sometimes even develops into a friendship," she continued. "In this job, you are constantly learning new things and going into situations that are interesting."

Being an interpreter is not always fun, however. "Sometimes you are in over your head because of many factors," explained Sally. "Patients are occasionally embarrassed or don't want you there. Or an impatient doctor or nurse mumbles everything. Sometimes the phone rings with an assignment at the worst possible time, but you still have to drop everything and go anyway."

The lives of interpreters are often full of change. One week, you might be working in a hospital. The next week, you might be in a courtroom or at a business meeting. Being able to adapt to different kinds of environments is important. You need to really be a "people person" to succeed. Interpreting is all about working with people and understanding what they have to say to each other.

Red Cross volunteers need to communicate with one another and with the people they help.

In recent years, the American Red Cross has put an emphasis on providing volunteer interpreters at disaster sites around the world. They joined with the American Translators Association (ATA) to do this. ATA former president Marian Greenfield recently said, "In times of crisis, when human communication can be a matter of life and death, ATA's interpreters will be on the front lines working hand-in-hand with the American Red Cross to support disaster relief efforts."

Many interpreters work for agencies that employ several interpreters. But more than 22 percent of interpreters are self-employed. This allows them to set their own hours and fees. They are usually paid by the hour. Sometimes they are paid a specific amount for a whole project.

As an interpreter, you need a number of important traits. A successful interpreter must:

- be patient
- be punctual
- be a careful listener

- be a clear communicator
- be flexible with his or her time
- have an excellent memory
- have an extensive vocabulary
- pay very close attention to conversation without getting distracted
- be able to do independent research on terms and common phrases that will be needed on each individual job

Having confidence in yourself helps others have confidence in you.

The way an interpreter dresses and behaves is an important part of doing a good job. Part of being professional is to look professional. Most interpreters wear a suit or dress pants and a shirt to a job. They speak politely and do their best to inspire trust and confidence in their clients.

LIFE & CAREER SKILLS

Many careers require a professional attitude and appearance. Interpreters must pay extra careful attention to this. They are communicating the words and ideas of people other than themselves. Because of this, they must make sure their own thoughts and opinions do not interfere. The interpreter must be as accurate as possible in translating the client's words. Otherwise, the people the client is talking to might misunderstand.

CHAPTER THREE
GETTING TRAINED, GETTING CERTIFIED

You will need special training if you want to work as an interpreter. You can get this training at many colleges. You can also attend conferences and special workshops.

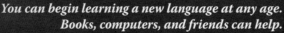

You can begin learning a new language at any age. Books, computers, and friends can help.

Learning how to speak at least two languages extremely well is the most important skill you will need. Some people are raised **bilingual**, meaning they grow up speaking two languages in their house. Others first get the chance to learn a foreign language in high school. It is a great way to get started. Interpreters usually have at least a bachelor's degree from a college. The degree does not have to be in language. It can be in other areas like English, computer technology, or education.

Many interpreters encourage students to live in a foreign country for a while. Even if it is only for a short time, doing so will be helpful. It gives students a chance to hear and use the language on a fluent, native level. It also teaches them the slang and terms people use on a daily basis.

What if you can't live in a foreign country? There are other ways to learn a language on a native level. One is reading books and magazines in that language. Another is getting an **internship** with an interpreting agency. You can learn on the job by working on projects and talking to your coworkers.

Most interpreters are certified. This means that they have passed certain tests. They have the necessary training to do a skillful and trustworthy job. The certification a person gets depends on what kind of interpreting is required. Interpreters who work in the federal courtroom might get certification in speaking Spanish, Navajo, and Haitian Creole. State and local courts sometimes have their own forms of certification. Sign language interpreters have their own specific tests.

There are two main types of interpreting. Both help people but in slightly different ways.

The first type is called **consecutive** interpreting. This is what is used when people are working one-on-one. It is used by interpreters in medical offices or when

Interpreters help representatives from many countries communicate as if they were all speaking the same language.

they work as guides to foreign visitors. In consecutive interpreting, a person speaks while the interpreter listens very carefully. He takes notes on what is being said. When the person finishes, he repeats what has been said in the other language.

The second type of interpreting is **simultaneous**. It takes longer to learn and requires more skill. In this style, the interpreter listens to one language as it is being spoken. He must instantly translate it in his own mind and then repeat it aloud. As the interpreter is speaking the words, the first person is often still talking. Simultaneous interpreting requires the ability to listen and talk at the same time.

Simultaneous interpreting is used in the United Nations. Interpreters sit in soundproof booths. They wear headphones over their ears and listen to one language. Then they translate what they hear into the microphone in front of them. This is relayed to a listener's headphones. This way, when a representative speaks in his native language, those from other countries understand right away what he is saying.

Courtrooms use this type of interpreting also. As a witness testifies, an interpreter listens and translates the words to the judge and jury. When attorneys ask a question, the interpreter immediately translates it to the witness so he can reply. These interpreters are also often present at attorney–client meetings, hearings, and sentencing.

LEARNING & INNOVATION SKILLS

Have you ever seen someone use sign language? Specific finger and hand movements are used in place of spoken words. The way the interpreter holds his body, the expressions on his face, and how he moves his hands reflect the words and the feelings behind them. American Sign Language (ASL) is used to talk to people who are hearing impaired. ASL interpreters are always in demand. Sign language interpreters are used in schools across the country, as well as in hospitals, courts, and government offices. What skills do you think you would need to become a sign language interpreter?

In either type of interpreting, it is very important to know the special terms people use. If you do not know medical terms or legal terms, it is easy to get confused. Interpreting takes a lot of practice and patience. Just knowing how to speak the languages is not enough. It calls for fast thinking and an amazing ability to multitask!

An ASL interpreter sometimes stands beside a speaker. That way, everyone can see what he is signing.

CHAPTER FOUR
INTO THE FUTURE

When the United States was attacked on September 11, 2001, Americans across the country realized

Interpreters in Iraq help soldiers from other countries work closely with local police.

An interpreter can make it possible for someone's story to be heard.

many important things about this nation. One of them was that it had a severe lack of qualified interpreters, especially those who spoke Arabic. When witnesses, victims, and criminals who spoke Arabic were brought into the U.S. court system, there were not enough people who could interpret for them. Since then, leaders have focused on helping more students pursue careers in interpreting.

Do you think you would like to be an interpreter? The good news is that you will probably have no trouble finding a job.

Experts predict that interpreters will be in high demand at least through 2016. Many will be needed in the medical world. Others will be needed in work that is related to homeland security. The need for the most common languages, often referred to as PFIGS (Portuguese, French, Italian, German, and Spanish) will stay steady. The need for other languages such as Arabic, Chinese, Korean, Japanese, Russian, Farsi, and Pashto will grow. The need for qualified sign language interpreters is also increasing.

LIFE & CAREER SKILLS

You need to understand your personal strengths to decide on a career. If you are interested in becoming an interpreter, ask yourself these questions: Do you deal well with stress and pressure? Can you do more than one thing at a time? Do you adapt easily to being in different places and with different people? Can you speak clearly and slowly? Do you have a large vocabulary? What about a good memory? Can you think quickly on your feet? Are you a "people person"? If you answered yes to most of these questions, you may have what it takes to succeed as an interpreter.

Interpreters help people work together to discuss issues and make decisions.

The nation's largest cities, such as Washington, D.C., Los Angeles, and New York, will be the best places to find work. Sign language interpreters will be needed in almost all communities, however.

How much interpreters are paid depends on many different factors. How many languages do you speak? What subjects are you familiar with? What kinds of skills and certification do you have? Who have you worked with before? Do you have recommendations from other employers? All of these factors can affect how much you are paid. In 2006, the average hourly pay was about $17. Those who work with the federal government can earn more than $76,000 a year. Highly skilled interpreters can make more than $100,000 a year.

If you choose to become an interpreter, your goal will be helping people understand one another. Maybe you will help patients communicate with doctors. You might explain legal terms to witnesses in courtrooms. Perhaps you will change words from lectures into sign language. You might even help government officials interview suspected terrorists. No matter what kind of interpreting you choose, you will be part of an exciting, rewarding, and cool career!

SOME FAMOUS INTERPRETERS

Svetlana Guggenheim (1966–) was born and raised in Moscow. She is currently based in Washington, DC. She has done extensive freelance interpreting for federal agencies, corporations such as Lockheed Martin, organizations such as Doctors Without Borders, and many private individuals. She is passionate about her work and believes that dedicated interpreters never stop learning and perfecting their skills. Her favorite quote is from Johann Wolfgang von Goethe, who said, "He who does not know foreign languages does not know anything about his own."

Doña Marina (c. 1501–c. 1527), also known as Malinche, was a Mayan slave. She worked with Hernán Cortés as he traveled the world, conquering lands. Since he only spoke Spanish, he could not ask for food or directions, negotiate terms, or make agreements with the people he met of the different cultures. Doña Marina helped him communicate with the native tribes.

Sacagawea (c. 1788–1812) joined the Lewis and Clark expedition in 1804. She was the only woman among 33 men. During the trip, she gave birth to her son and carried him on her back. She served as an interpreter to many of the Native American tribes they met on their northwestern journey. Often it was her presence that convinced the tribes that the explorers were friendly.

Anne Sullivan (1866–1936) is perhaps one of the most famous interpreters. She became the teacher of Helen Keller, who was blind, deaf, and mute. Through the use of sign language spelled directly into Keller's hand, she was able to help Keller learn about the world, go to college, and communicate with people.

GLOSSARY

bilingual (bye-LING-gwuhl) speaking two languages fluently

conquistador (kuhn-KEE-sta-door) a Spanish conqueror

consecutive (kuhn-SEK-yuh-tiv) following one after another without a break; a style of interpreting where one person speaks and then the other follows

hieroglyph (HYE-ruh-gliff) a picture writing symbol used by the ancient Egyptians

internship (IN-turn-ship) an opportunity for students to work with experts in their field of interest and learn more about careers they are thinking about pursuing

simultaneous (sye-muhl-TAY-nee-uhss) happening at the same time; a style of interpreting where a person translates at the same time he or she is listening

FOR MORE INFORMATION

BOOKS

Miller, Sarah. *Miss Spitfire: Reaching Helen Keller.* New York: Atheneum Books for Young Readers, 2007.

Summitt, April R. *Sacagawea: A Biography.* Westport, CT: Greenwood Press, 2008.

West, David, and Jackie Gaff. *Hernán Cortés: The Life of a Spanish Conquistador.* New York: Rosen Publishing Group, 2005.

WEB SITES

Discover Interpreting
www.discoverinterpreting.com/
Videos of interpreters talking about their work and more information on careers in interpreting

National Association of Judiciary Interpreters and Translators
www.najit.org
Information about interpreting and translating in legal settings, including a list of frequently asked questions

National Council on Interpreting in Health Care
www.ncihc.org
Learn more about health care interpreting

INDEX

ABOUT THE AUTHOR

Tamra B. Orr is a full-time author living in the beautiful Pacific Northwest. She has written more than 150 books for readers of all ages and learns something new every single time. She is mother to four and earned her degree from Ball State University. In her rare spare time, she likes to read, write old-fashioned letters, and visit the coast with her family.